DATE DUE

MAY 1 4 2011	
FEB 2 0 2012	
MAY 0 8 2012	
JUL 0 6 2012	
JUL 1 6 2012	
DEC 0 3 2012	
MAY 2 5 2013	
JUL 1 9 2013	
APR 3 0 2014	
JUL 0 3 2014	
AUG 2 1 2014	
SEP 0 4 2014	

BRODART, CO.   Cat. No. 23-221

Super Simple
Things to Do with
Water
Fun and Easy Science for Kids

Kelly Doudna

Consulting Editor, Diane Craig, M.A./Reading Specialist

A Division of ABDO

ABDO
Publishing Company

To Adult Helpers

Learning about science is fun and simple to do. There are just a few things to remember to keep kids safe. Be sure to review the activities before starting, and be ready to assist your budding scientist when necessary.

Also, encourage your child to clean up. Materials should go back where they belong! Finally, when using food coloring, be careful not to stain counter tops and clothing.

visit us at www.abdopublishing.com

Published by ABDO Publishing Company, a division of ABDO, P.O. Box 398166, Minneapolis, Minnesota 55439. Copyright © 2011 by Abdo Consulting Group, Inc. International copyrights reserved in all countries. No part of this book may be reproduced in any form without written permission from the publisher. Super SandCastle™ is a trademark and logo of ABDO Publishing Company.

Printed in the United States of America, North Mankato, Minnesota
102010
012011

 PRINTED ON RECYCLED PAPER

Editor: Liz Salzmann
Content Developer: Nancy Tuminelly
Cover and Interior Design and Production: Oona Gaarder-Juntti, Mighty Media, Inc.
Photo Credits: Kelly Doudna, Shutterstock
The following manufacturers/names appearing in this book are trademarks: Dawn®, McCormick®, Morton®, Pyrex®

Library of Congress Cataloging-in-Publication Data
Doudna, Kelly, 1963-
  Super simple things to do with water : fun and easy science for kids / Kelly Doudna.
    p. cm. -- (Super simple science)
  ISBN 978-1-61714-677-0
  1. Water--Experiments--Juvenile literature. 2. Science--Experiments--Juvenile literature. I. Title.
QD169.W3D68 2011
546'.22078--dc22
                        2010021087

Super SandCastle™ books are created by a team of professional educators, reading specialists, and content developers around five essential components—phonemic awareness, phonics, vocabulary, text comprehension, and fluency—to assist young readers as they develop reading skills and strategies and increase their general knowledge. All books are written, reviewed, and leveled for guided reading, early reading intervention, and Accelerated Reader® programs for use in shared, guided, and independent reading and writing activities to support a balanced approach to literacy instruction.

Contents

Super Simple Science

Want to be a scientist? You can do it. It's super simple! Science is in things all around your house. Science is in a bottle and in stones. Science is in pepper and in dish soap. Science is even in salt and in food coloring. Science is everywhere. Try the **activities** in this book. You will find science right at home!

Water

Learning about science using water is super simple! Science explains why water flows. Science explains why an index card can seal water inside a bottle. Science can even keep different colors of water from mixing together. In this book, you will see how water can help you learn about science.

Work Like a Scientist

Scientists have a special way of working. It is a series of steps called the Scientific Method. Follow the steps to work like a scientist.

1. Look at something. Watch it. What do you see? What does it do?

2. Think of a question about the thing you are watching. What is it like? Why is it like that? How did it get that way?

3. Try to answer your question.

4. Do a test to find out if you are right. Write down what happened.

5. Think about it. Were you right? Why or why not?

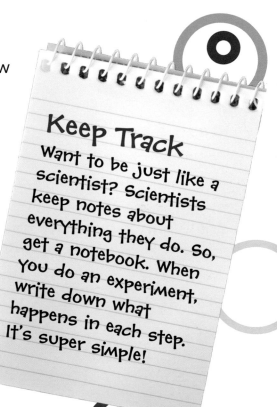

Keep Track

Want to be just like a scientist? Scientists keep notes about everything they do. So, get a notebook. When you do an experiment, write down what happens in each step. It's super simple!

5

Materials

baking pan

stack of books

1-liter plastic bottle and cap

handkerchief

flexible tube

large stones

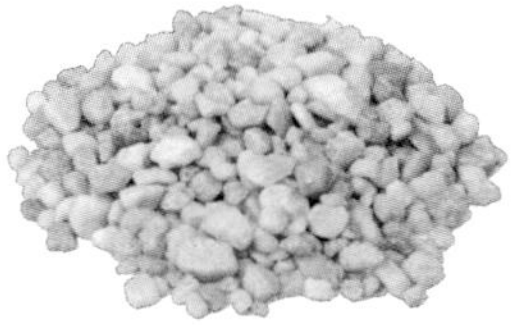

small stones

pitcher

food coloring

clear straw

measuring cup

wooden matchsticks

small jars

index cards

salt

ground pepper

clear plastic cups

liquid dish soap

large screw

measuring spoons

tall glasses

pencil & paper

Bottled Up

Water will leak out of a hole, right?

Removing the cap allows water to leak out the hole.

What You'll Need
- baking pan
- empty 1-liter plastic bottle and cap
- large screw or nail
- water

Poke a hole near the bottom of the bottle with the screw.

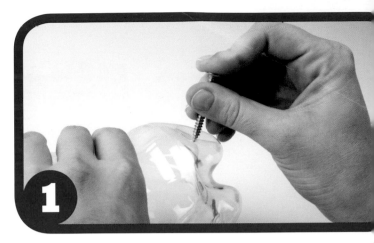

 Hold your finger over the hole. Fill the bottle with water. Screw on the cap.

3 Hold the bottle over the baking dish. Slowly remove your finger from the hole. Try not to **squeeze** the bottle with your other hand. Does anything happen?

4 Unscrew the cap. What happens now?

What's Going On?

When the cap is on the bottle, air pressure can't push down on the water inside the bottle. So the water does not **leak** out. But when you unscrew the cap, air pushes into the bottle. The water streams out of the hole.

Super Simple Siphon

Can you move water from one glass to another without pouring?

What You'll Need
- 2 glasses that are the same
- 12-inch (30 cm) flexible tube
- stack of books
- water

Water flows through the tube until the level is the same in both glasses.

Doudna — It's K! — ABDO

Gaarder-Juntti — What Lives in the Desert? — ABDO

What Has Wings?

Salzmann — Alley to Zippy — ABDO

Lindeen/Doucet — GRIZ FINDS GOLD A Story About California — ABDO

Kenney — Super Simple Glass Jar Art — ABDO

1 Fill both glasses half full with water. Put one end of the tube into one of the glasses.

2 Suck on the other end of the tube just until the water fills the tube.

3 Remove the tube from your mouth, quickly putting your finger over the end. There should be little or no air in the tube. Put the covered end into the other glass of water. Remove your finger.

4 Place one glass on the pile of books. What happens to the water level?

5 **Switch** the glasses. Now what happens?

What's Going On?

Air pressure pushes down on the water. That causes water from the upper glass to flow into the lower glass until the levels are even. When you switch the two glasses, the levels even out again.

Pack It In

Do small and large stones take up the same amount of space?

What You'll Need
- pitcher
- 2 glasses that are the same
- small stones
- large stones
- water
- measuring cup
- pencil and paper

There is less empty space between the small stones.

There is more empty space between the stones.

1 Fill one glass with small stones. Fill the other glass with large stones. Fill both glasses to the top with water.

2 Pour the water from the glass of large stones into the measuring cup. Hold the stones in the glass with your fingers. Write down how much water you poured out.

3 Empty the measuring cup. Pour the water from the glass of small stones into the measuring cup. Write down how much water you poured out of the glass.

4 Are the two amounts of water the same? Are they different? Why do you think this is?

What's Going On?

The glass with large stones holds a little more water than the glass with small stones. That's because there is more room between the stones. The small stones are packed more tightly. There is less room in between for water.

Expand Your Horizon

Can a drop of soap push pepper and move matches?

What You'll Need
- baking pan
- water
- ground pepper
- liquid dish soap
- wooden matchsticks

The soap spreads out on the water. It pushes the pepper and matches away.

Part 1

1 Fill the baking pan with water about 1 inch (2.5 cm) deep.

2 Sprinkle several shakes of pepper into the water.

3 Put one drop of dish soap in the middle of the pepper.

4 What happens?

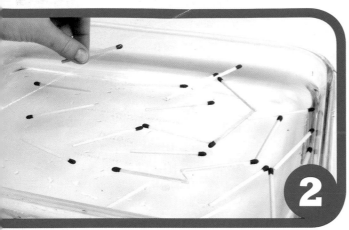

Part 2

 1 Empty and rinse the baking pan. Fill it again with 1 inch (2.5 cm) of water.

2 Put 40 wooden matchsticks in the water. They can touch, but they should not be on top of each other.

 3 Put one drop of dish soap into the middle of the matchsticks.

4 What happens?

What's Going On?

The pepper sits on the surface of the water. When a drop of soap hits the water, a thin **layer** of soap spreads out over the surface of the water. The soap pushes the pepper away. The same thing happens with the matchsticks, even though they are bigger.

16

Sealed Up Tight

How many ways can you hold water in?

Thin layers of water on the card and cloth keep water from spilling.

17

Part 1

1 Put the cloth over the glass. Use your finger to push it into the glass. Fill the glass most of the way with water.

2 Slowly pull the cloth down the outside of the glass. Pull until it is tight across the top of the glass.

3 Put one hand over the top of the glass. Turn the glass over with your other hand. Hold it over the baking pan, just in case.

4 Slowly move your hand away from the glass. What happens?

18

Part 2

 Fill the jar with water all the way to the top.

 Put the index card over the mouth of the jar. Hold it there as you turn the jar upside down.

 Hold the jar over the cake pan, just in case. Remove the hand that's holding the index card. What happens?

 Try shaking the jar gently. Does the card stay in place?

What's Going On?

When the cloth gets wet, water clings to small spaces between threads. This creates a thin **layer** of water on the cloth. It keeps the rest of the water from **leaking** out of the glass. A layer of water also forms on the index card. It holds the card to the jar and keeps the water in.

19

Straw Pole

Do yellow and blue always make green?

Adding salt changes the **density** of the water. Different colors don't mix.

1 Fill each cup with water. Add 10 drops of a different food coloring to each cup.

2 Going from left to right, add salt to each cup. Add 1 teaspoon (5 ml) to the first cup. Add 2 teaspoons (10 ml) to the second cup. Add 3 teaspoons (15 ml) to the third cup. Add 4 teaspoons (20 ml) to the fourth cup.

3 Stir each cup until the salt **dissolves**.

4 Once again, go from left to right. Stick one end of the straw about 1 inch (2.5 cm) into the first cup. Put your finger over the other end of the straw. Take the straw out of the cup. A little water is held inside the straw.

5 Keep your finger over the end of the straw. Hold it straight up and down. Stick it 2 inches (5 cm) into the second cup. Slowly remove your finger from the end. Then put your finger back over the end of the straw.

6 Remove the straw and stick it 3 inches (7.6 cm) into the third cup. Slowly remove your finger. Put your finger back over the end of the straw.

7 Remove the straw and stick it 4 inches (10 cm) into the fourth cup. Slowly remove your finger. Put your finger back over the end of the straw.

8 Pull the straw out. Have the colors mixed? Or are they still separate?

Part 2

1 Fill the two jars almost full with water.

2 Add 10 drops of yellow food coloring to one jar. Add 10 drops of blue food coloring to the other.

3 Add 1 teaspoon (5 ml) of salt to the yellow jar. Add 2 teaspoons (10 ml) of salt to the blue jar. Stir each jar until the salt **dissolves**.

4 Put the jars in the baking pan, just in case. Add more water to the jars so that they are **completely** full.

5 Place the index card over the yellow jar. Hold it there as you turn the jar upside down.

6 Set the yellow jar on top of the blue jar. Keep the index card between them. Line up the jar rims.

7 Have a helper hold the jars. Slowly pull the index card out from between them. What happens?

What's Going On?

When you add salt to water, you increase its **density**. Density affects how much the water floats or sinks. The water that has the least salt floats at the top. The water that has the most salt stays at the bottom.

Conclusion

Congratulations! You found out that science can be super simple! And, you did it using water. Keep your thinking cap on. How else can you experiment using water?

Glossary

activity – something you do for fun or to learn about something.

completely – entirely or in every way.

congratulations – something you say to someone who has done well or accomplished something.

density – how heavy something is for its size.

dissolve – to mix with a liquid so that it becomes part of the liquid.

layer – one thickness of a material or a substance lying over or under another.

leak – to get in or out of something through a small crack or hole.

squeeze – to press the sides of something together.

switch – to change places or take turns.